Short ish Walks
The South Devon Coast

Paul White

Bossiney Books • Exeter

The approximate locations of the walks in this book

All the walks in this book were checked prior to printing, at which time the instructions were correct. However, changes can occur in the countryside over which neither the author nor the publishers have any control. Please let us know if you encounter any serious problems.

This updated reprint published 2022 by Bossiney Books Ltd,
68 Thorndale Courts, Whitycombe Way, Exeter, EX4 2NY
First published 2008
www.bossineybooks.com

© 2008 Paul White All rights reserved
ISBN 978-1-915664-06-8

Acknowledgements

We are grateful to Robert Hesketh for checking the walks prior to this edition. The maps are by Graham Hallowell. The photographs on pages 1, 7, 11 and 27 are by Robert Hesketh, www.roberthesketh.co.uk. All other photographs are by the author. Cover based on a design by Heards Design Partnership.
The boots on the front cover were kindly supplied by The Brasher Boot Company.

Printed in Great Britain by Booths Print, Penryn, Cornwall

Introduction

These 'shortish' circular walks range from 5 to 10 km (3¼ to 6¼ miles) and typically take 2 to 3 hours. The exact time will vary according to your fitness, weather conditions (take your time if it is slippery underfoot) and above all how interested you are in what you see. The duration times given make no allowance for this, as it is such a variable.

The area covered is the coast from Turnchapel, on the edge of Plymouth, round to Dartmouth. All the walks involve a section of the coast path with a rural outward journey or return, giving some idea of the countryside which backs this magnificent coast.

The scenery is fantastic, and full of geological interest. In summer, you are likely to see sailing craft in profusion, and you will often have a grandstand view of yacht races.

Comfort and safety

Inland country walking involves some mud at most times of the year, and after heavy rain, a lot of mud! You will also inevitably from time to time encounter farm animals, ill-maintained gates and damaged signposts, but on the whole this area is very walker-friendly.

I strongly recommend walking boots, not just because of the mud but to give ankle support. I also find a walking pole invaluable when descending the steeper parts of the coast path. Cliffs are exposed to the wind, so you may well find you need an extra layer or two, as well as a waterproof. Carry water with you (dehydration makes you tired) and some spare food.

The two obvious hazards are firstly the cliff paths, especially where the coast is eroding. They are unfenced, so children and dogs should be supervised. Secondly, traffic: where lanes are used, they are on the whole quiet, but care is nevertheless needed.

A less obvious hazard is ticks, which can cause Lyme disease. For this reason, and also because inland footpaths may be overgrown with nettles and other vicious vegetation, I strongly recommend you do not walk bare-legged when away from the coast path.

Whilst I doubt that you will get lost on these walks, our sketch maps only cover the route of the walk itself. The OS Explorer map OL20 (double-sided) covers this whole coast and is excellent value.

Paul White

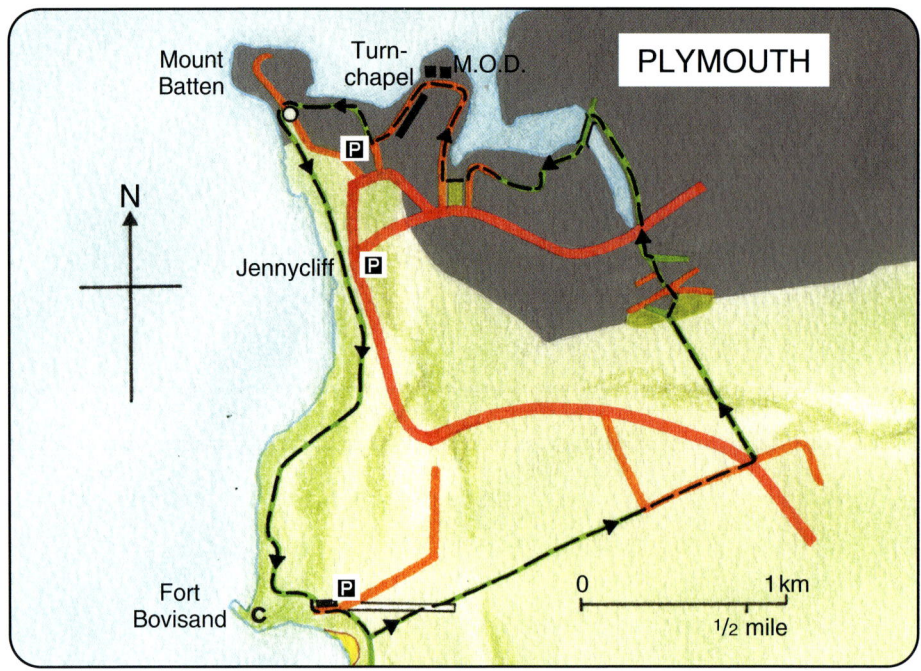

Walk 1 Bovisand and Turnchapel

Distance: 9.5 km (6 miles) Time: 2 3/4 hours
Character: A fascinating mixture of views over Plymouth Sound, a surprisingly rural section, then a generally interesting and attractive route through waterside areas of the city. Fairly easy walking, apart from a few flights of steps on the coast path near the start.

Start from the Jennycliff car park (free, SX 493524). (Alternatively, there are free car parks at Bovisand and Turnchapel.)

In front of you is a green area, with benches and a café. Turn left across the front of the benches and pick up a beaten path. This is soon identified as the coast path (POOLE 175 1/2 MILES). It winds through woodland, with several short flights of steps, then leads round to Fort Bovisand with its quay. Continue ahead down more steps, cross a footbridge, then turn left up a lane.

At the far end of a car park, bear right on the coast path, HEYBROOK BAY. At the foot of the steps, turn left on a footpath at a waymark. Follow it up the valley, crossing a private drive on the way (PUBLIC FOOTPATH STADDISCOMBE). Reaching a lane, continue ahead. When the lane reaches a more major road, continue ahead but after just 25 m turn left, then immediately left again up steps, PUBLIC FOOTPATH.

Continue in the same direction till you go through a kissing gate into a wood. Keep left, then after 100m at a fingerpost turn *right* (RED ROUTE). This path descends via steps. Cross two streets to a footpath just behind the REDDICLIFF CLOSE sign and zig-zag down. Pass the end of a close and continue down to a T-junction of paths.

Turn left, and follow the Erme-Plym Trail. Within a bit of open ground, the path turns right. Cross the main road into parkland. Bear right at the kissing gate to walk with the stream, and later the lake, on your left. Turn left across the dam and follow the path around the treatment works. At a fingerpost, turn sharp right for the coast path (red coast path signs). Turn right down a street, pass the Royal Oak and follow coast path signs around an inlet, out round the point and past MOD buildings.

It looks unpromising but there is a pedestrian gate at the end leading into Turnchapel village (photograph above) with its attractive late 18th and early 19th century cottages. Turn left at the Clovelly Bay Inn, past a chapel 'restored 1879'. At the top of the hill, turn right through a car park, SOUTH-WEST COAST PATH CLOVELLY BAY. You will reach the Plymouth Yacht Haven, at the neck of the Mount Batten peninsula.

You might want to walk out to the point (views over the Barbican, Citadel and Hoe) but otherwise walk up to the roundabout, cross the road and take the coast path left, which leads back to the start.

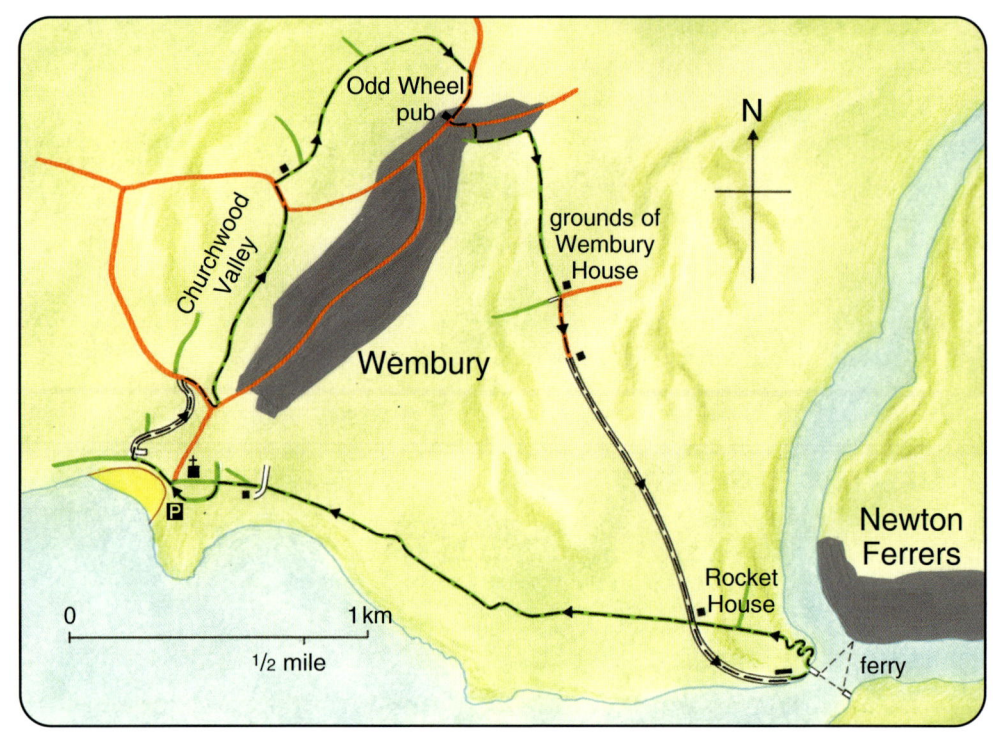

Walk 2 Wembury

Distance: 7km (4½ miles)   Time: 2 hours
(Can be shortened by 1km, cutting out a steep descent and ascent.)
Character: South Devon farmland and coast path, with views over the Yealm estuary at Warren Point. Could be connected, using the seasonal ferry, with Walk 3. Apart from the optional visit to the ferry, fairly easy walking.

Start from the car park at Wembury beach (SX 518485). Walk west across the back of the beach and over a footbridge. Turn immediately right, ERME PLYM TRAIL. Follow the path beside the brook. Do not cross the footbridge ahead. Reaching a lane, turn right.

You might want to explore the National Trust's Mill Meadow on the left. Otherwise, walk past and, at the road junction, turn sharp left on PUBLIC BRIDLEWAY. At a lane, turn left, then turn right after 50 m, HIGHER FORD FARM. Keep right at a path junction, climb and cross fields. Keep right at another junction, then follow the footpath when it bears right across a field.

Reaching a lane, turn right. At the Odd Wheel, turn left. Opposite

the shops, turn right into PUBLIC FOOTPATH. At a path junction, turn left then shortly right up steps. Follow the well-beaten path (signed ALLOTMENTS) past the allotments and Wembury House, then turn right on a tarmac lane, which later becomes a track, LINK TO COAST PATH. At length this leads to a gate, by the old rocket house, where you have a choice of turning right immediately (in which case, skip the next paragraph) or walking down to the ferry. And back up! There are good views on the way.

A gentle descent down the track leads to cottages and the ferry, which is seasonal and has varying hours, so check return times if using it. You can either return up the same track, or, just 5 m beyond the ferry access, turn left up a footpath – there are steps which zigzag up, so it is considerably more demanding than the track but very scenic. Either way will bring you back to the rocket house.

Then take the coast path, WEMBURY. Just before Wembury church, turn left and continue to the car park.

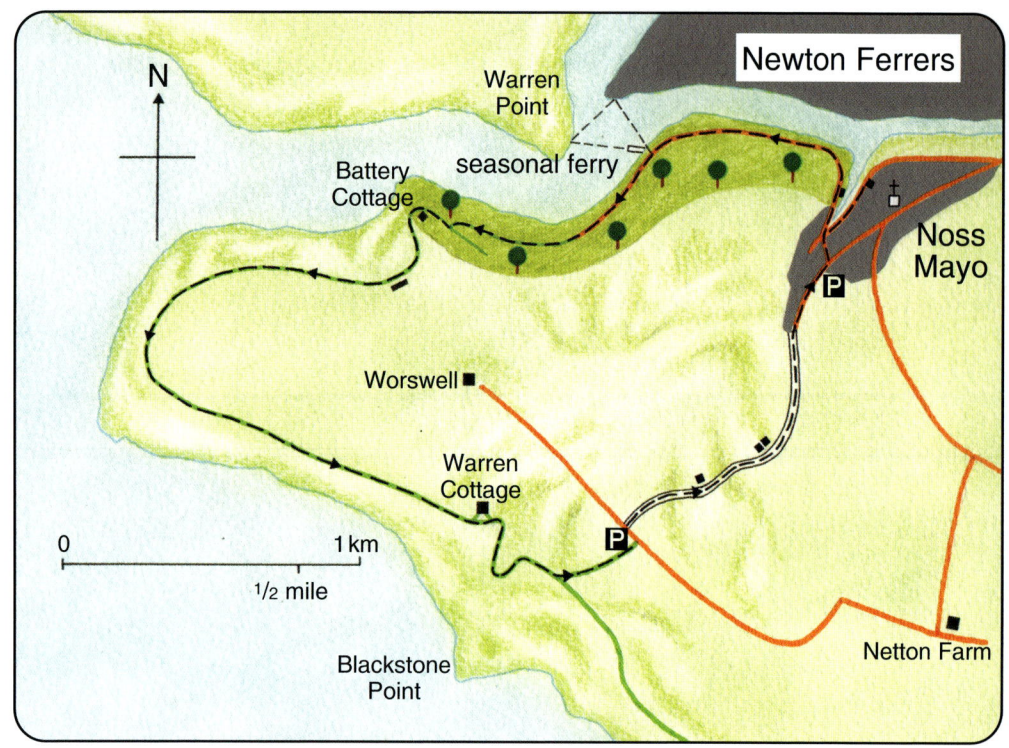

Walk 3 Noss Mayo

Distance: 6.8km (4¼ miles)   Time: 2 hours
Character: An easy walk, with gentle gradients but a great variety of scenery, from open farmland at the start, down to the creekside village of Noss Mayo, along the wooded creekside, then a stretch of coast path on National Trust land.

Noss has a famously picturesque setting, and like its neighbour across the creek, Newton Ferrers, has gone up and up in the world's (and particularly estate agents') estimation. A century of development, especially in Newton, and in recent decades the growth of second home and boat ownership, have made them ideal places for the well-keeled.

Start from the National Trust's Warren car park. (To get there, follow signs to Noss Mayo. Keep left up to the church. At the church, keep left again. Take a right turning for NETTON and WORSWELL. Pass Netton Farm and turn right, WORSWELL.)

From the car park, turn left along the lane and then almost immediately right, PUBLIC FOOTPATH NOSS MAYO. This is mostly a broad stony track and leads into the village past tennis courts and a car park. Bear

left just beyond the bus turning area, down to the village hall and the Tilly Institute.

Divert briefly along Creekside Road for views, and the Swan Inn. Then return to the Tilly Institute and turn right, this time past the Ship Inn. Continue along the lane, which curves left. Turn left up steps, FORDHILL PLANTATION. Follow the footpath ahead parallel to the lane. Continue until the path dips to rejoin the lane.

Walk ahead, COAST PATH THE WARREN. The path soon divides. Keep right, COASTPATH. The footpath joins a stony track. Keep left when the track divides (the path right leads only to the beach). Continue to a gate and along the Coastpath (Revelstoke Drive). Continue as the Coastpath turns south and then east. Keep left at a fingerpost PUBLIC FOOTPATH WARREN NOSS MAYO. Follow it back to the car park.

Lord Revelstoke

Edward Baring (1828-1897), First Baron Revelstoke, was a third-generation merchant banker who did everything on the grand scale, including buying the 1600 hectare Membland Estate.

His financial dealings were utterly reckless, and Barings had to be rescued by a Bank of England loan. Revelstoke was disgraced and his personal assets were sold, but his son turned the disaster around and the bank remained solvent.

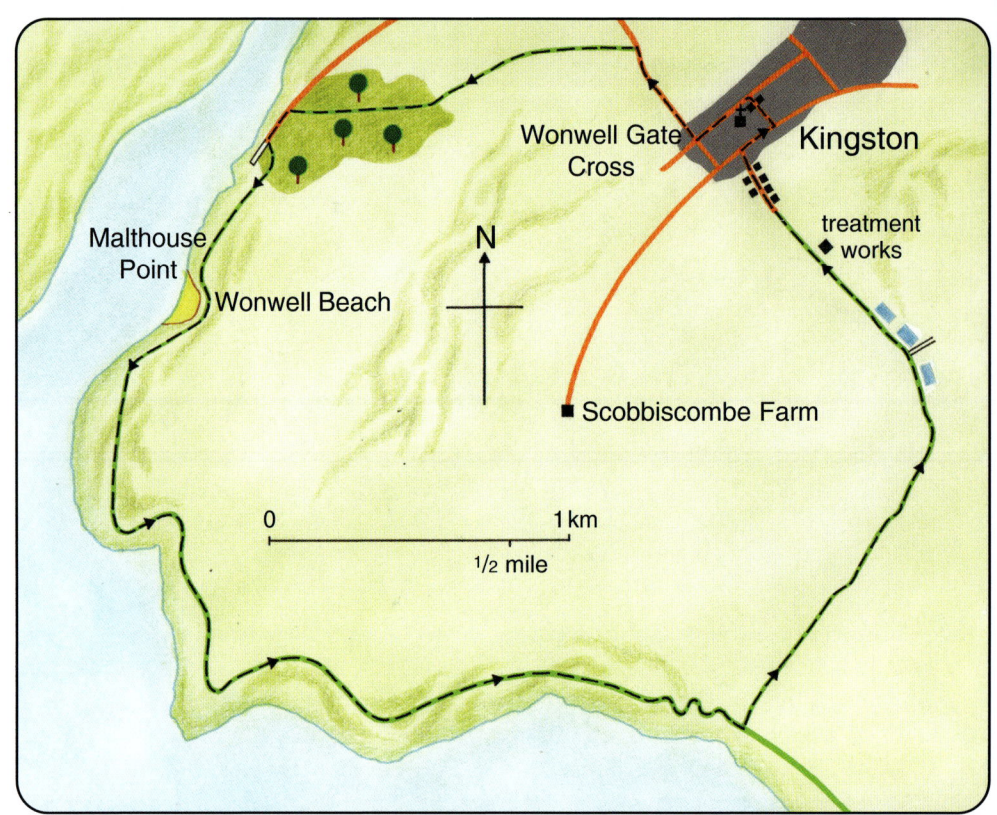

Walk 4 Kingston and the Erme estuary

Distance: 9km (5½ miles)   Time: 3 hours
Character: Attractive inland and coastal scenery, relatively easy walking throughout except for one steep descent. A short stretch of quiet lane, then footpaths and bridleways throughout. If you consider combining this walk with Walk 5, be aware that the intervening coast path section involves very steep ascents and descents.

There is usually parking at Kingston near the church (SX 635478). Starting from the Dolphin Inn, turn left past the church and walk up to Wonwell Gate Cross. Turn right along a lane. After 400m turn left, PUBLIC FOOTPATH. This crosses fields then descends through a wood.

Reaching a lane, turn left. Just after it becomes a track, turn left, COAST PATH BIGBURY-ON-SEA.

The path initially runs beside the estuary, with attractive views inland, then turns left along the coast.

By coast path standards it is not too hilly and makes for steady walking. Pass through a wicket gate beside a large concrete cattle trough, and climb to Hoist Point, where there is a granite bench. Continue along the path, which suddenly descends steeply.

At the foot, just before a wooden footbridge, turn left inland, KINGSTON. The path crosses a stream then passes through a wood. At a junction, bear right PUBLIC BRIDLEWAY KINGSTON. Pass a series of pools on your right, continuing up the left side of the valley. These are in fact downstream from a treatment works, but when I walked this way there were no unpleasant odours.

After gently gaining height over a distance of more than 2 km (would that all uphill paths were as gentle!) the bridleway arrives at the edge of Kingston and becomes a lane. Follow this up to a T-junction.

Turn right, then first left and you will find the sixteenth-century Dolphin Inn on either side of the road.

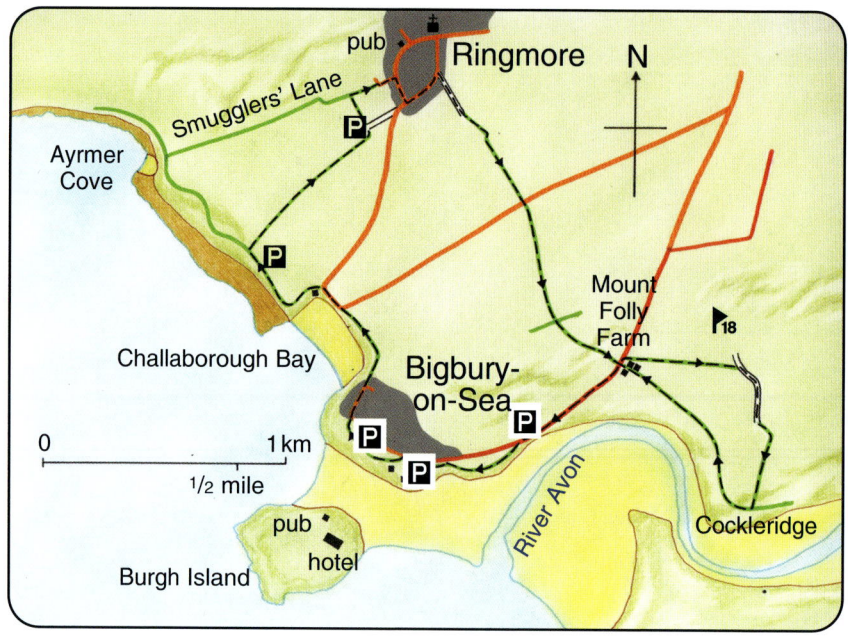

Walk 5 Ringmore and Bigbury

*Distance: 8 km (5 miles) but can be shortened   Time: 2½ hours
Character: Attractive countryside and coastal walking, mainly on footpaths. Several fairly steep ascents and descents. The optional visit to Ayrmer Cove involves a steep descent.*

Start from the National Trust Ayrmer Cove car park at Ringmore (SX 650456), contributions requested. Leave by the AYRMER COVE exit. After 100 m, turn right, VILLAGE and JOURNEY'S END. Follow a path, then a lane. At a T-junction, to explore the village and locate the Journey's End pub, turn left, but for the walk turn right.

At a T-junction turn left past Challaborough Cottages. Turn right into a lane, signed as a dead end. At the end, take the PUBLIC FOOTPATH, then continue in the same direction, PUBLIC FOOTPATH, to cross the valley. Descend and follow the path across a stream and up the other side. Cross a lane and then another valley.

Reaching a ridge, continue ahead as signed. On reaching the road at Mount Folly Farm, turn left and after 50 m turn right, PUBLIC FOOTPATH. (You could omit the visit to Cockleridge, saving 2.1 km and one ascent, but you would miss some lovely views over to Bantham and down the Avon estuary to Burgh Island.)

Keep the hedge on your right to the end of the field, and go through

a gate into a golf course. Continue till you reach a tarmac drive, then turn right, PUBLIC FOOTPATH. Where indicated, turn left through a gate. Keep the hedge on your left round two sides of a field and continue down to the shore of the estuary. Turn right BIGBURY-ON-SEA and follow the path back up to Mount Folly.

Cross the road. Turn left and follow COASTPATH downhill, parallel to the road along the field edge. After 550 m, re-cross the road. Turn left and follow the gravelled path parallel to the road down to the beach. A further diversion from the road (COASTPATH) brings you to a massive car park, where there are toilets, a café, a shop and the possibility of visiting Burgh Island.

The coast path follows the lane past the car park, then through an overspill car park, then briefly a lane, COAST PATH CHALLABOROUGH, then a path. Pass Challaborough Bay Holiday Park, turn left at the recycling bank, COAST PATH. Continue ahead, COAST PATH WONWELL. At a junction of paths you have a choice. Either turn right, RINGMORE, along the near-level path to the car park, or, if you still have a bit of spare energy, continue on the coast path.

Descend steeply to Ayrmer Cove, a lovely spot beautifully maintained by the National Trust, then turn first right up the valley by a huge stone. Follow Smugglers' Lane as it climbs gently. At the top, turn right for the car park or straight on for the Journey's End.

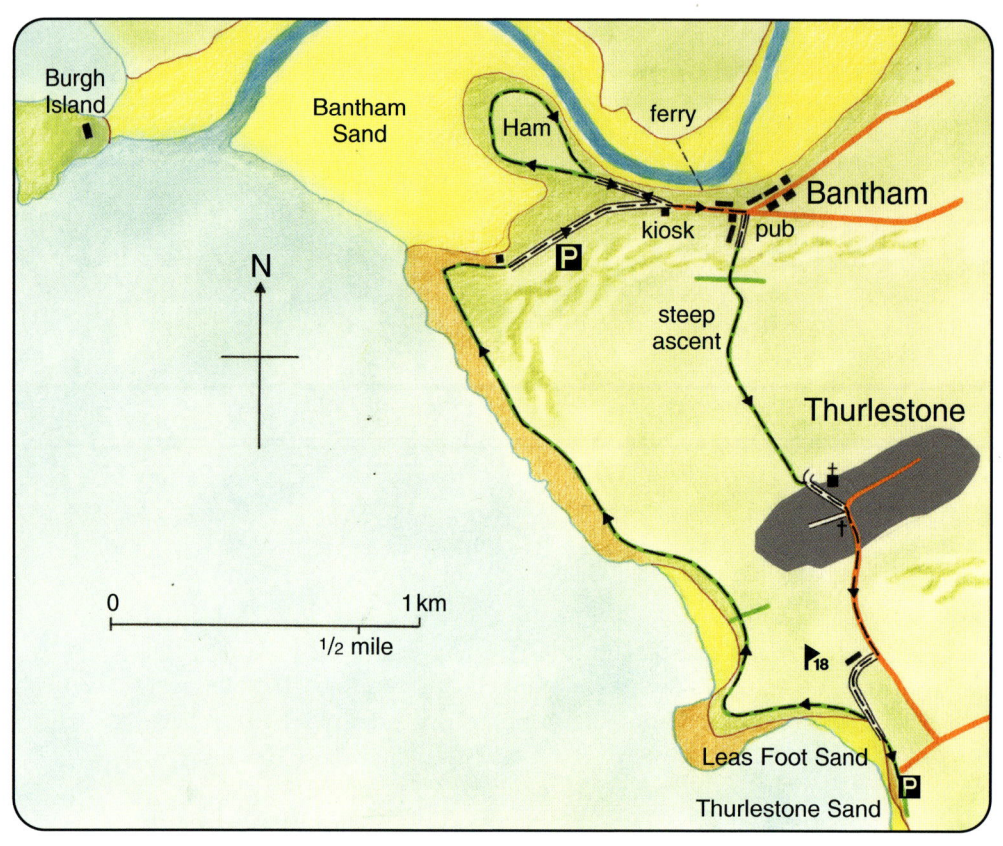

Walk 6   Thurlestone and Bantham

Distance: 7.5km (4½ miles)   Time: 2 hours
Character: A popular walk along the cliff path with wonderful views of Burgh Island and the coast, then an exploration of an area of dune and beach. You could equally start from the Bantham beach car park. One steep ascent, but mostly easy walking on well trodden paths.

Start from the car park at the north end of Thurlestone Sand (SX676420). Facing the sea, turn right along COAST PATH PUBLIC BRIDLEWAY. Follow the path when it diverts along the cliff top, and continue along it to Bantham Sand.

When the tide is out, you can take a short cut across the beach to Bantham Ham. Otherwise, follow COAST PATH BIGBURY VIA SEASONAL FERRY through the beach car park. At the ticket kiosk at the entrance to the car park, turn sharp left to explore the dune area.

If you omit the exploration of the dune area, you will cut the total walk distance by 1.6km, a mile.

From the ticket kiosk, continue up the lane to the Sloop Inn, bear right then immediately turn right beside the inn, PUBLIC FOOTPATH. At the foot of a slope, turn left, cut across the field and turn right on a well-beaten path up a steep hill. (May I recommend the view to your right, best seen from about two thirds of the way up, and well worth stopping for!)

Follow yellow waymarks to Thurlestone. Pass the church on your left. At the war memorial and village green, continue ahead down the lane, past tennis courts. Turn right on a driveway past the Golf Club and then retrace your steps to the car park.

Right: The Burgh Island sea tractor works from Bigbury at high tide

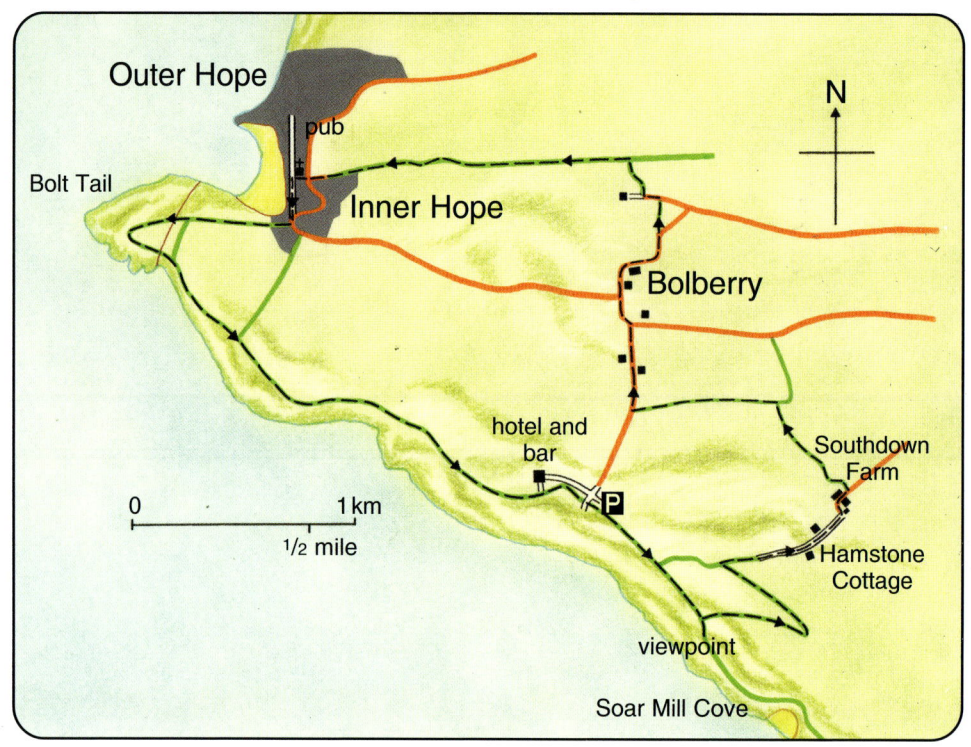

Walk 7 Bolberry and Hope Cove

Distance: 10.25 km (6 1/4 miles) Time: 3 1/4 hours
(Could be cut to 6.5 km by walking up the lane from the car park.)
Character: A lovely mix of farmland and coast, visiting the old fishing village of Inner Hope and the prehistoric promontory fort on Bolt Tail, which may have sheltered the locals in time of war, or perhaps been a trading post for foreign merchants. One steep descent near the start, but the ascents are gentle to moderate. Could be combined with Walk 8 to make an all-day walk.

Start from the National Trust Bolberry Down car park (SX 690385). Facing the sea, turn left through the car park and pick up the coast path. At the sign indicating CATHOLE CLIFF, carry on for 100 m for the view, then retrace your steps to the sign and take the path inland, descending steeply. The path may be a little overgrown and muddy at some times of year. At the foot, turn left into South Down Farm and follow the beaten path gently uphill through fields to a T-junction.

Turn right, MALBOROUGH. The track leads up to and through Southdown Farm, which has been developed for National Trust holiday

accommodation. Leaving the farm, turn left, PUBLIC FOOTPATH and follow the yellow waymarks and footpath signs round the farm buildings and along the side of a field. At the end of the field, turn left, BOLBERRY DOWN.

On reaching a lane, turn right. At the T-junction turn left, HOPE COVE. Take special care round the bend. At the next junction bear right downhill. Climb a slope and continue ahead, UNMETALLED ROAD. Turn left at a T-junction and after 80 m (after passing through a gate signed 'Higher Barton') turn right up four steps, PUBLIC FOOTPATH GALMPTON, and follow waymarks.

At the field at the end of the path, turn right. Go through a metal gate and then turn left at a waymark post. This broad track continues in roughly the same direction for 1.25 km, then becomes a lane. Cross a road (or turn right for the Hope & Anchor pub) into the footpath past St Clements church, then turn left onto the coast path.

Cross behind the beach (diverting left if you want to explore Inner Hope) then take the steps beside the lifeboat house (COAST PATH SALCOMBE). The path leads up to the entrance of the Bolt Tail promontory fort.

Climb to the highest point to enjoy the views, then turn and follow the path with the sea on your right. After about 2.5 km you will reach the Bolberry Down car park.

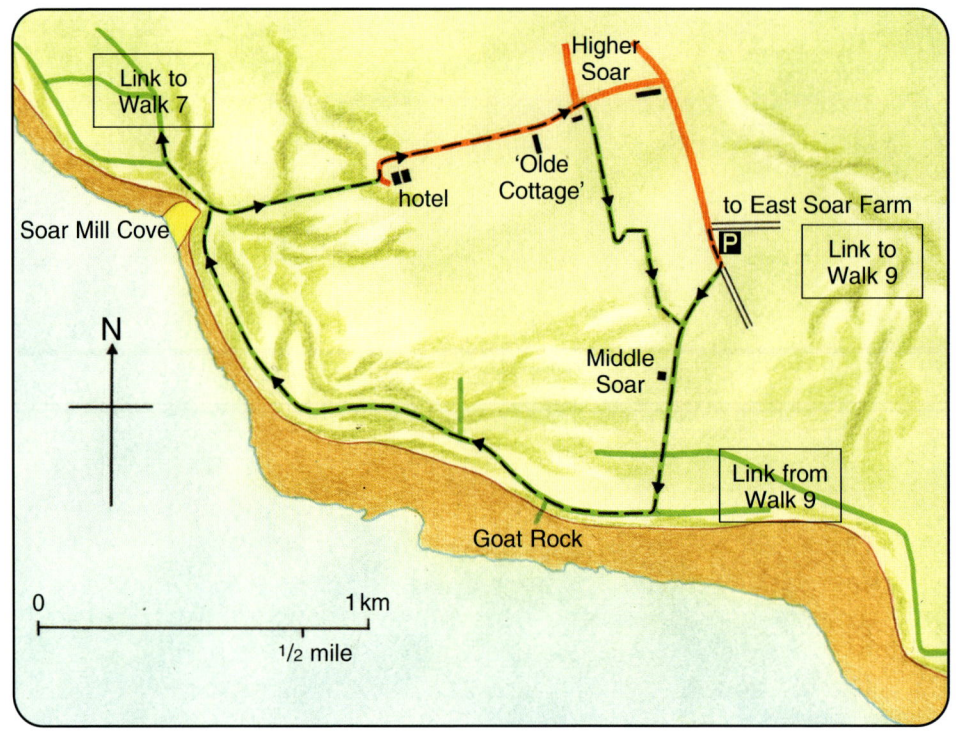

Walk 8   Soar Mill Cove

Distance: 5.4km (3½ miles)   Time: 1½ hours
Character: A short walk but with lovely cliff scenery and a delightful sandy cove to visit. Mostly footpaths with one short section of narrow lane giving access to the beach and a hotel. One steep descent. Could be combined with either Walk 7 or Walk 9.

Start from the National Trust car park at East Soar (SX713375). To get there, head towards Salcombe on A381. At Malborough, turn right GALMPTON BOLBERRY SOAR. Just past the church, keep left, BOLBERRY SOAR, then follow signs for SOAR. At a crossing, by former coastguard houses, continue ahead to the car park.

From the car park, continue ahead on the lane by which you arrived, LINK TO COASTPATH SOAR MILL COVE. After 100m, turn right, PUBLIC FOOTPATH. Skirt around Middle Soar as signed and continue ahead. At a path walk ahead, LINK TO THE COASTPATH. Turn right onto the Coastpath. At a path crossing, continue ahead, acorn waymark. A gate leads out on to the cliffs. Turn right SOAR MILL COVE. A headland

on the left (GOAT ROCK) provides extensive views. Continue along the Coastpath until it descends to sandy Soar Mill Cove.

To link with Walk 7, turn left BOLBERRY BOLT TAIL then at the next junction fork right (LOWER PATH TO BOLBERRY) and continue up the valley to the signed entrance into Southdown Farm.

Otherwise, turn right for MALBOROUGH and ascend steadily. The well concealed buildings of Soar Mill Cove Hotel come into view. Keep to the left of them and join a lane. Pass the car park and then Lower Soar, with its attractive thatched 'Olde Cottage'. Ignore PUBLIC FOOTPATH LINK TO COASTPATH.

At a mind-blowingly complex road layout – not so much a Spaghetti, more of a Vermicelli Junction, which had a motorist utterly confused even as I walked past – turn right onto PUBLIC FOOTPATH.

The path goes through two gates. Continue along the field edge ahead to the field corner. Turn left. Turn right at the yellow waymark 100 m ahead round a tight dog-leg, then continue south-south-east as signed, along the grassy bank that marks the field boundary, to a gate. Go through the gate and walk ahead 50 m to another waymark. Turn left on the path and retrace your steps to the car park.

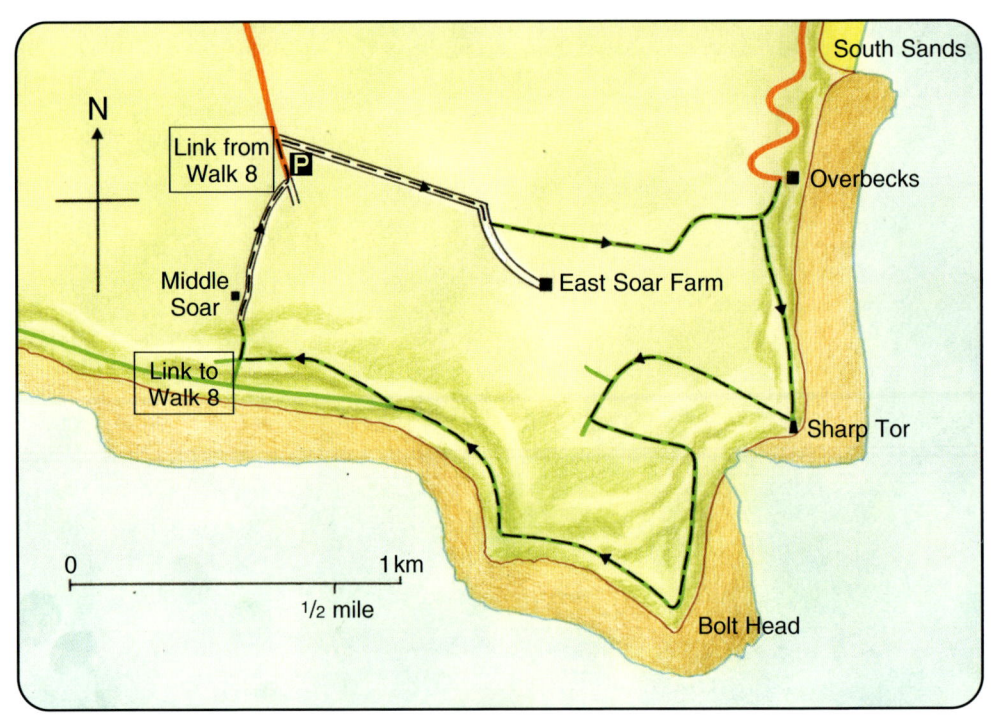

Walk 9 Overbecks and Bolt Head

Distance: 6.4km (4 miles)   Time: 2 hours
Character: Stunning views of coast and estuary. Mainly easy walking, though with a couple of moderate ascents. Could be combined with Walk 8.

Start from the National Trust car park at East Soar (SX713375). See Walk 8 for directions for getting to this car park.

From the car park, take the track signed OVERBECKS. Soar was, you might think appropriately from its name, a wartime airfield, RAF Bolt Head. It still has a landing strip. According to the 1946 one-inch OS map, however, the farms were then called Sewer, not Soar, and there was a Sewer Mill Sand where now there is Soar Mill Cove. By what process, I wonder, were the historic names changed? Certainly it is an improvement!

The track turns right. Turn left for OVERBECKS, across fields. At a fingerpost, turn left, OVERBECKS, going through two gates to walk with the fence on your left. At the next junction carry straight on, OVERBECKS DIRECT. Go through another gate. Either continue ahead to visit Overbecks, or turn right up steps and follow the path ahead.

Views of the estuary open up, especially from Sharp Tor. The path then winds down, to cross a stream. Go through the gate and turn left down the slope. Continue ahead at a waymark, then again at the SOAR MILL COVE sign. When the path forks, bear right MIDDLE SOAR SOAR MILL COVE, diverging from the Coastpath.

Reaching another junction, turn right, MALBOROUGH (unless you want to link with Walk 8, in which case you should continue along the cliff path). Continue ahead at a path junction, MALBOROUGH. Pass to the right of Middle Soar and continue up the access track till you reach a tarmac lane. Turn left back to the start.

Overbecks

This National Trust property has a microclimate perfectly suiting the rare and exotic species in its garden, which can be enjoyed against spectacular background views. The house of the former owner, chemist Otto Overbeck (1860-1937) is currently closed.

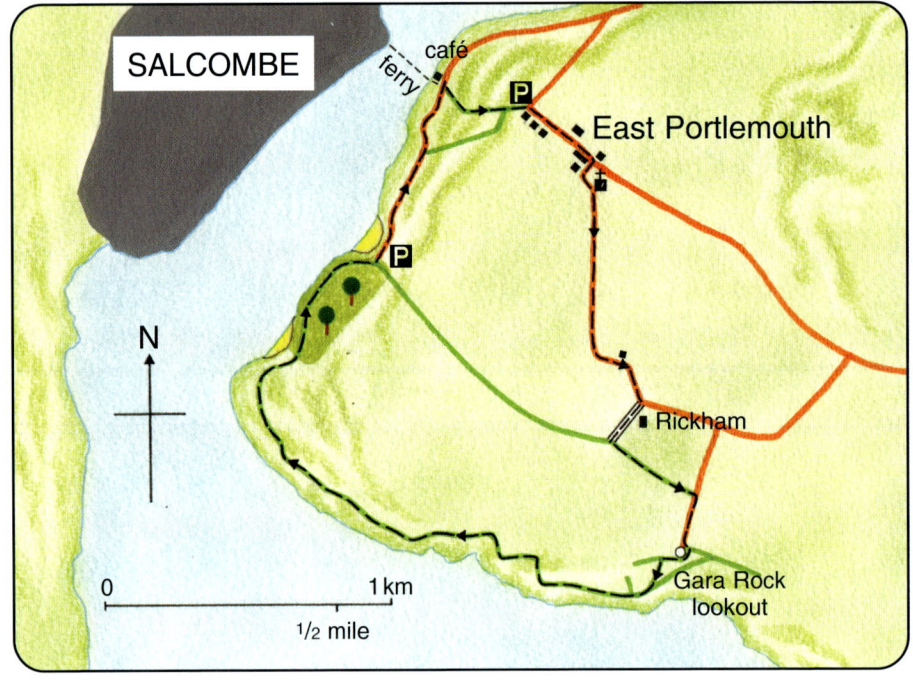

Walk 10   East Portlemouth

Distance: 6km (3 3/4 miles)   Time: 1 3/4 hours
Character: A short inland stretch on very quiet lanes leads to the coast path at Gara Rock. The path provides lovely views as you approach Salcombe Harbour. It is uneven at one point, where it runs near the cliff, and vertigo sufferers might have a problem with it. There is also one steep ascent, from the ferry to the village.

The passenger ferry from Salcombe, which operates in the summer months, would make an ideal start for this walk – but do check the time of the last return ferry of the day.

If arriving by car in East Portlemouth, there is a parking area downhill from the church, at the top of 'Passageway', which is the bridleway between the village and the ferry.

From the parking area, walk uphill to the church, and turn right on the lane to RICKHAM. Turn right down the NO THROUGH ROAD and follow the track up into the trees, then turn left (PUBLIC FOOTPATH) onto a path. After crossing two fields, cross a track and go through the gate opposite, then turn right down a lane, past the Gara Rock development, which includes a café (limited hours).

At the end of the lane is the Gara Rock lookout. Turn left, then after 20m right, COAST PATH MILLBAY. Keep left at a fork, then right at the waymark to join the coast path (i.e. the more scenic lower path). Follow it round to a National Trust car park (busy in season, so not a good place to start the walk).

From this point a narrow lane leads ahead, to the ferry, where the Venus café provides refreshment for waiting passengers.

Turn inland almost opposite the café up PUBLIC BRIDLEWAY EAST PORTLEMOUTH. At a junction, continue ahead, EAST PORTLEMOUTH.

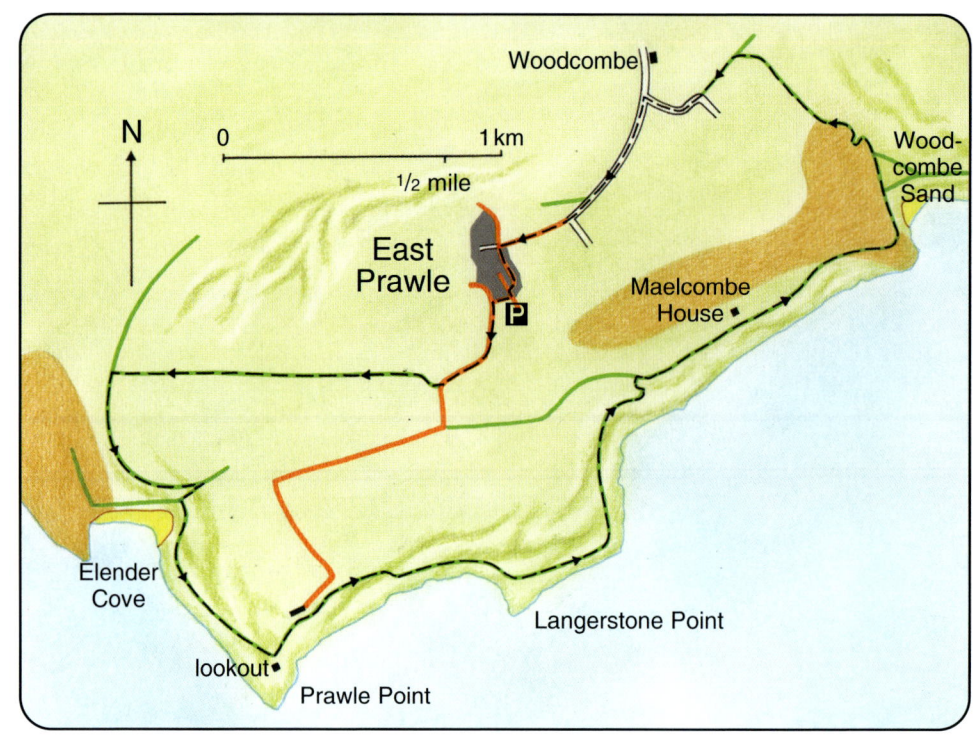

Walk 11   East Prawle

Distance: 8.75km (5½ miles)   Time: 3 hours
Character: A classic blend of beautiful coast and South Hams farmland. Whilst much of the walk is easy, there are two steep ascents, and a couple of places where the coast path is uneven and rocky, running near the cliff edge – we think it unsuitable for dogs. The walk can also be quite muddy in places.

The remote village of East Prawle has a free village parking area around a green (SX 781364) and supports a pub and a café, not to mention public toilets. BUT the parking area can be busy, especially at weekends.

From the parking area, walk down the PUBLIC BYWAY, also signed for walkers PRAWLE POINT. Where the lane turns left, continue ahead PUBLIC BRIDLEWAY. After 1.25km, turn left at a T-junction, down towards Elender Cove (see photograph opposite), one of the most beautiful on this stretch of coast.

At the waymarked path junction, turn right down to the Coastpath – the descent is steep and may be slippery if wet. Turn left along the Coastpath.

Initially deceptively easy, the following few hundred metres are really difficult going, climbing over rocks. But it will get easier later! When you reach the National Coastwatch lookout post at Prawle Point (Devon's most southerly point) turn left to pass in front of a terrace of houses. Now continue along the coast path for 2 km.

When you reach a field where the path doubles back on itself, ignore the first path on the right (signed with a blue arrow) and take the second path right – the Coastpath. After you pass Maelcombe House, the craggy cliffs get ever closer and ever more bizarre. You will again need to watch your step since the path becomes rocky and uneven as it rounds Woodcombe Point.

At the Woodcombe Sand waymark, continue ahead and at the next junction keep left, uphill, EAST PRAWLE. The path is both steep and at times muddy. Ignore side turnings. At a T-junction of paths, turn left, PUBLIC BRIDLEWAY. Join a track, follow it round a right turn, then turn left, PUBLIC BRIDLEWAY.

Ignore a blue waymarked turn and follow the track, later a lane, to a T-junction within the village. Turn left and follow a lane which wriggles around past property entrances, to a T-junction. Turn left, then first right, back to the start.

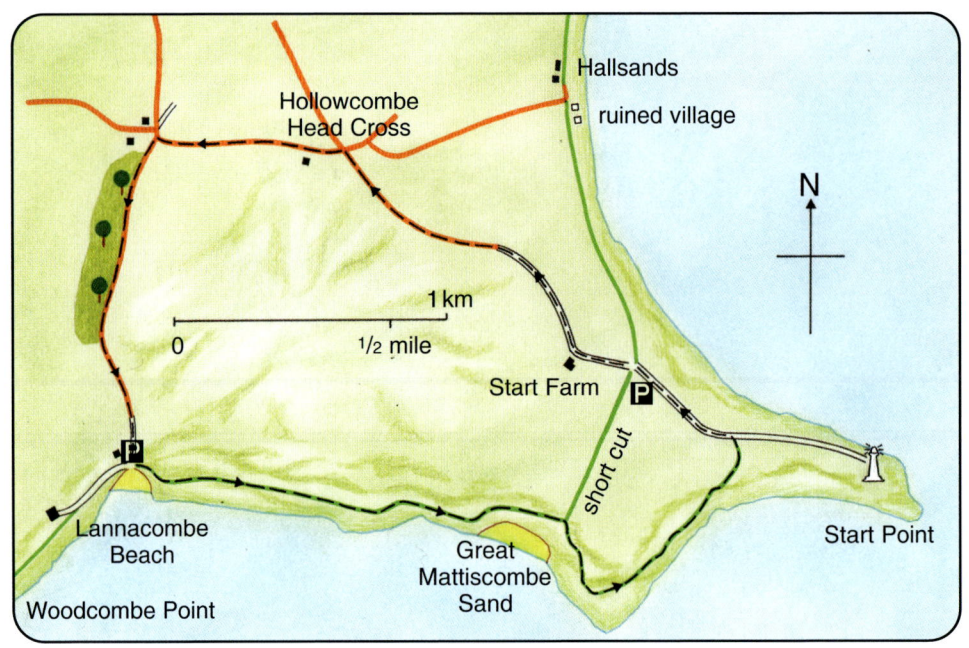

Walk 12 Start Point

Distance: 6.8km (4¼ miles)   Time: 2 hours
Character: An easy walk which gets better and better as it proceeds. After a modest start, it descends into a lovely valley, then heads out to the coast path for some remarkable cliff scenery. There is more tarmac than in most of our walks, but the lanes are quiet and very attractive.

   The coast path from Lannacombe to Great Mattiscombe Sand is easy walking. From there to Start Point is uneven but there is an easy short cut which avoids this section. There are possible short extensions in either direction, both with fairly easy walking. This walk could be combined with either Walk 11 or Walk 13 to make a full day's walking.

   There are several tempting beaches on this walk, so if tide and temperature are suitable, go prepared.

Park at the Start Point car park (SX 821375). Begin by walking back along the access drive, past Start Farm and the radio masts, and then continue to Hollowcombe Head Cross. Turn left, LANNACOMBE, and descend to a road junction. Take the first left and walk seaward to Lannacombe Beach.

   You might want to divert right for a closer look at the remarkable rocky outcrops on Woodcombe Point, for comparison with Start

Point itself. Otherwise turn left along the coast path. This is an eroding coast, so please take notice of warning signs and diversions. At a path junction, you could take the left turn back to the car park, or turn right. This section of the coast path does need care and is not recommended to vertigo sufferers.

Nearing Start Point, the path climbs to the crest of the ridge. Just over the top is the lighthouse access drive, and you could divert down to the lighthouse which is 500m away. Otherwise, turn left up the tarmac driveway which leads to the car park.

Hallsands is about 1 km (2/3 mile) away down the coast path to the north – a gentle descent and easy walking.

> Hallsands in the nineteenth century was a fishing village with 37 houses, protected from the sea by a pebble beach. When, in the 1890s, the Admiralty wanted to expand Plymouth's dockyards, they gave permission for the shingle to be dredged. Despite protests, the dredging went ahead. By 1900 damage to the village was evident, but dredging continued. In 1917 storms destroyed all but one of the houses. The compensation offered to the homeless villagers collectively was just £6000.

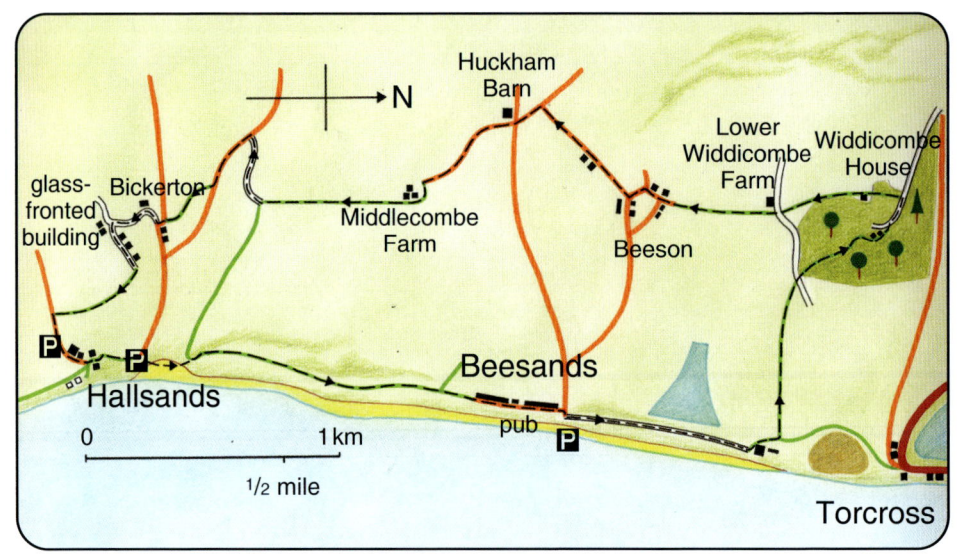

Walk 13 Beesands and Hallsands

Distance: 8.2 km (5 1/4 miles)   Time: 2 3/4 hours
Character: A contrast of coast and countryside – shingle beaches at Beesands and Hallsands, undemanding coast path between – and on the inland route both farmland and the outskirts of a landscaped estate. Some footpaths may be a bit overgrown, so bare legs could be a real liability.

Start from Beesands, where there is normally plenty of parking. (Alternatively, you could start from Hallsands.) Facing the sea, turn left (north) along the back of the beach and past a lake. At the end of the beach access track, turn left to pass behind a substantial white house, then turn left again, PUBLIC FOOTPATH.

Go through a gate into a large field. Keep the hedge on your left to the very end of the field, then turn right as signed and go through two gates into woodland. Keep right past houses, then continue on a private drive signed PUBLIC FOOTPATH.

After a further 250 m, turn left at a waymark. Follow waymarks. Emerging from the grounds of Widdicombe House, descend a field with a wall on your left. Go through a wooden gate at the bottom of the field, then follow PUBLIC FOOTPATH almost straight ahead, passing to the left of Lower Widdicombe Farm. Faced with two gates, take the one on the right.

Cross the valley bottom, join a track, bear right and you will arrive in Beeson. Continue ahead to a T-junction and turn left, BEESANDS, then after 100m (by 'Cobb Cottage' and 'Rose Cottage') turn right up a minor lane. Climb steadily to a T-junction. Turn left and then at Huckham Barn Cross continue ahead, FARM ONLY.

Reaching the farm gate, turn left down a footpath, PUBLIC WAY. Go through a gate beside barns, following red arrow waymarks, then through an unusually wide wooden gate into a footpath. Follow this down to a track. Ignore the footpath sign for Hallsands but take the track to a lane. Turn left, then after 150m turn right, BRIDGEWAY LANE BICKERTON. In Bickerton, bear right (see map) for Bickerton Farm, snaking down to PUBLIC FOOTPATH.

Turn left (PUBLIC FOOTPATH) when faced with a glass-fronted house. The track becomes a path, then emerges into a field. Keep the hedge, later a fence, on your left to the very end of the field. Cross a stile and turn left onto a lane.

At the top, after a diversion to the viewing platform for the ruined village, continue along the lane, which becomes a path. Go across the back of the beach and follow the coast path for BEESANDS.

At a junction, bear right (acorn waymark) back down to Beesands.

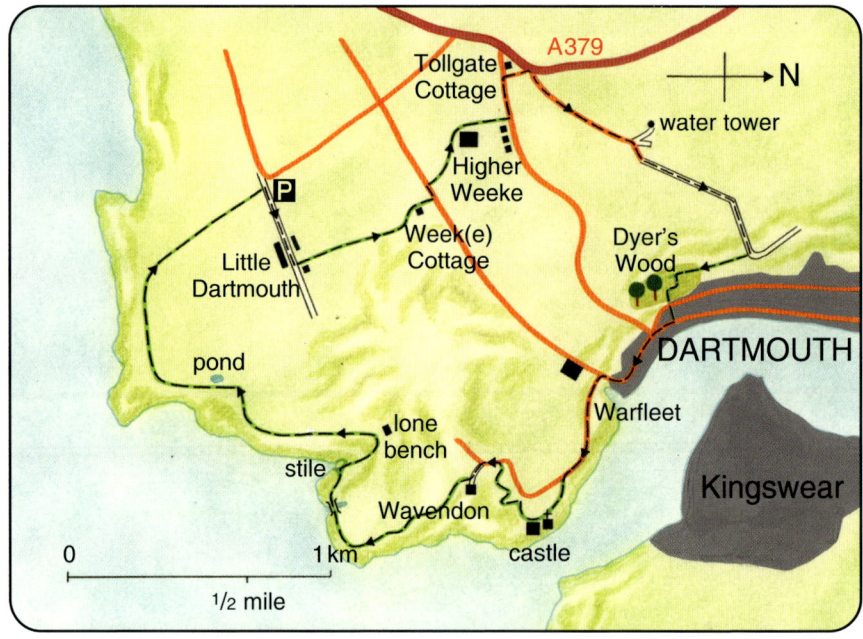

Walk 14 Around Dartmouth

Distance: 8km (5 miles) Time: 3 hours
Character: Initially quiet countryside, then wonderful views over the Dart estuary, and finally a dramatic stretch of coastline. Several ascents and descents steep enough for steps – and benches – to be provided.

Park at the NT car park at Little Dartmouth (SX 874491). With the coast at your back, turn right onto PUBLIC BRIDLEWAY DARTMOUTH CASTLE. Walk through Little Dartmouth farmyard and look out for a signpost on the left. Turn left and head for WEEK COTTAGE. Descend a hill, go through a gate to the left of Weeke Cottage and turn left when you reach the lane. After 50m turn right (PUBLIC FOOTPATH).

At a triple junction take the middle track, with a DIAMOND JUBILEE WAY waymark, and walk quietly past someone's living room to pick up the track again. Walk up a field to a lane and turn left. After 220m, turn right past Tollgate Cottage. Turn right onto the busy A379 for just 25m before keeping right onto the straight lane ahead – quiet except on a Sunday, when the recycling centre is open.

Just before you reach a tall water tower, turn right on a tarmac track (DIAMOND JUBILEE WAY) and head downhill towards the river. After about 700m, when the track takes a sharp left, turn right at a kissing gate, DIAMOND JUBILEE WAY. (NB this is the upper of two paths).

Continue into Dyers Wood, going through a gate and taking the path ahead. Then turn left down a flight of wooden-edged steps, which wind steeply down to a road – take care, they can be slippery. Cross and descend the flight of concrete steps opposite, down to a lower road. Turn right, then continue ahead into Warfleet Road. Turn left for DARTMOUTH CASTLE and cross a creek.

Keep left, and walk to the church and castle. Walk through to the tearooms and car park.

Now pick up the COAST PATH for STOKE FLEMING. You will notice its acorn waymarks all the way back to the car park, but there are a few unmarked junctions. The steps eventually wind and climb up to a road. Turn left, and immediately bear left again on the *lower* Coastpath by Compass Cottage. Pass to the right of 'Wavendon'.

The Coastpath emerges into the open at Blackstone Point, then hugs the open coast. When the tide is in and the sea rough this is very dramatic; in extreme weather conditions it would require caution. Reaching a tall fingerpost, turn right and follow the Coastpath as it curves inland and up a broad, very steep grassy track to a lone bench, at which point the path turns sharply left.

A short distance beyond a gate, the path forks. Keep left. In time you will reach a small pond. The path continues ahead to a field gate on the horizon. At the gate, turn right, and follow the broad grassy path, keeping a wall and then a fence to your right. When you reach a kissing gate, go through and follow the path uphill, back to your car.

Some other Bossiney walks books

Shortish walks on Dartmoor
Shortish walks – East Devon
Shortish walks near Exeter
Shortish walks – Lower Tamar Valley
Shortish walks – North Devon
Shortish walks – Torbay and Dartmouth

Dartmoor pub walks
Fairly easy walks on Dartmoor
Pushchair walks on Dartmoor
Really short walks – East Devon
Really short walks – South Devon
Really short walks to explore Dartmoor
South Devon dog walks
Walks on High Dartmoor
Writers' walks in Devon

Other Bossiney books which might be useful

101 things to see in Devon
Devon beach and cove guide
Devon's geology – an introduction
Exeter – a Shortish Guide.
Plymouth – a Shortish Guide.